MW01462425

Name: ______________________________

Contact: ______________________________

____

____

____

____

____

Year: ____________

FAT DOG
PUBLISHING

Published by Fat Dog Publishing in 2017

First edition; First printing

INDEX

Pages	Subject

INDEX

Pages	Subject

INDEX

Pages	Subject

Made in the USA
Thornton, CO
10/16/22 08:03:25

c5a89372-731b-411d-a7df-49185c2231e0R01